# MAGIC BLOOD

A Loving Reminder

Written by Sundari Grace
Illustrated by Camille Peyrard

© Sundari Grace 2019
First published in Australia in 2020 as this edition.

ISBN: 978-0-6485533-6-6 (Paperback)
ISBN: 978-0-6485533-7-3 (Hardcover)

All rights reserved. Apart from any fair dealing for the purposes of private study, research, criticism or review, as permitted under copyright law, no part of this book may be reproduced by any process without written permission. Inquiries should be addressed to info@sundarigrace.com.

Cover artwork and illustrations by Camille Peyrard

www.sundarigrace.com

for humans everywhere –
we were all fed by Magic Blood

# MAGIC BLOOD

A Loving Reminder

there's magic in this cup i hold

its power shines in cranberry bold

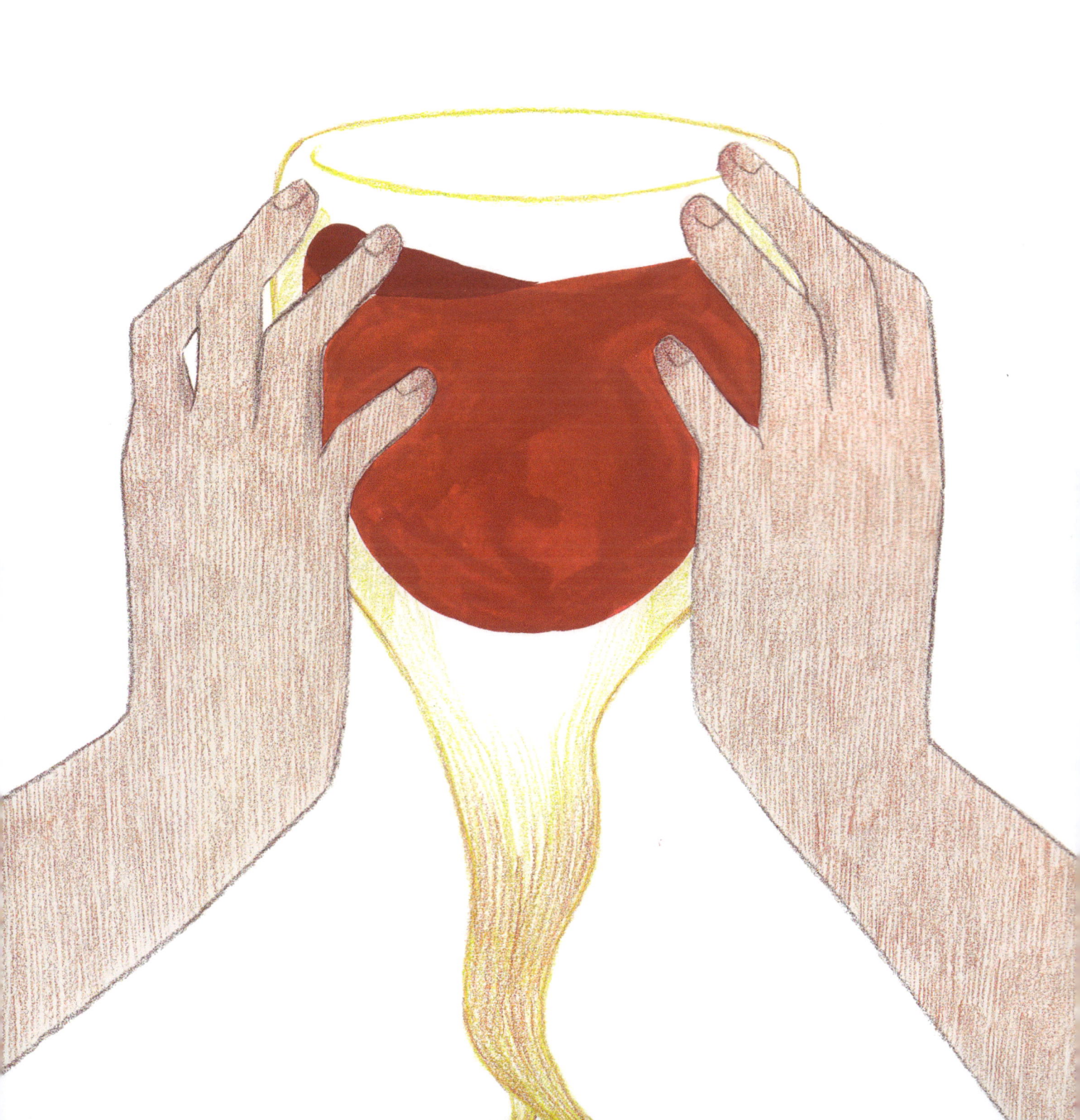

i marvel at its secret skill

to offer Life its growing fill

i love this earthen vessel mine

through which this magic blood doth shine

i love and softly care for it

while hormones, muscles do their bit

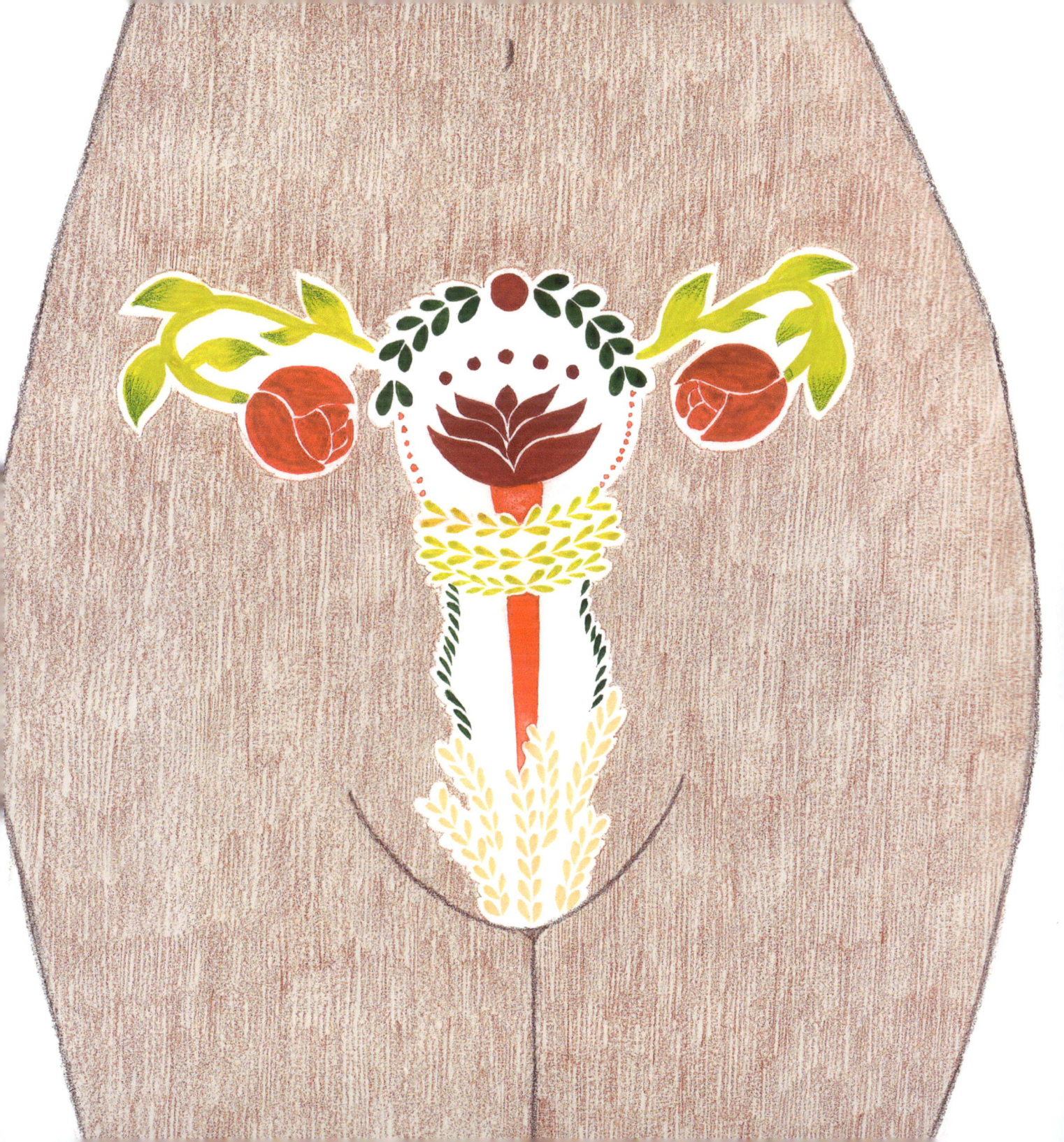

i thank the goddess, gods and crones

for pouring wonder through this flow

i ask that they might take this bud

and feed it with more magic blood

# About the Author

Originally from Melbourne, Australia, Sundari Grace has lived in Australia, the USA and Chile and now resides in sunny south-east Queensland. She started writing poetry and short stories in her early teens and has been on a lifelong journey of discovery ever since.

Sundari's writing reflects her deep and abiding interest in spirituality, sexuality and relationships as extreme sports that challenge and empower us to grow. She explores the light and shadow self, and the adventure of showing up in both – in solitude and interaction – to create opportunities to self-actualise and support each other to do so. Key themes in her writing include explorations of yearning, spiritual concepts of feminine/masculine, nature, beauty, energy, power and choice.

She draws on study and exploration in the fields of spirituality and literature, and is inspired by any experience that feels like jumping out of a plane.

www.ingramcontent.com/pod-product-compliance
Lightning Source LLC
Chambersburg PA
CBHW041431010526
44107CB00046B/1569